CALCULATE

YOUR

SAVINGS

LIZALYN SMITH

To my friends and family who listened to my ideas and encouraged me to complete this work, thank you.

I wrote Calculate Your Savings© to show you how to quickly identify the best ways to minimize your expenditures. I understand how it feels to be short on time and energy, and yet still want to be frugal. The strategies detailed here will show you how to choose where to get started. You can expect to learn how to gain a clear perspective of the best ways for YOU to become more frugal today. The journey to writing this book has been challenging, but I have learned a lot through trial and error. I have also become very efficient at judging which strategies are the best during the different seasons of life.

Contents

How This Book Works

In this day and time, there are countless blogs, vlogs, websites, books, and even television shows on frugality. I don't know anyone who has the time and patience to implement every frugal or thrifty strategy, but most people I know would love to save some money on household spending. Oftentimes, people try and force themselves to use popular strategies that seem to help others save money, but they end up frustrated when it does not work for them. This book is different because I show you how to determine which of the countless strategies are best for you by helping you quickly calculate what is required and decide whether it is truly worth your time. If you only have 30 minutes a day, or even one hour a week to dedicate solely to "being frugal," you will find something here that will help you begin your journey.

In order to decide which strategies are best for you, you must have a clear picture of what you typically spend on products or services. In Part 1, I show you how to quickly compare costs to benefits of a strategy, and then how to calculate how much you can save by using your best frugal strategies. Part 2 is dedicated to showing you how I implement the key strategies that make the biggest impact to my savings in my food spending.

Part I:
Calculate Your Savings©

Introduction: What is Frugal?

Cook meals from scratch! Use coupons! Have a garage sale! In our society, there are countless tips, tricks and strategies we can use to save money. How much do these strategies really save, and are the savings even worth the time?

Calculate Your Savings© is about becoming aware of the best frugal strategies for you and focusing your efforts on implementing them. There are many ways to save money in other areas of a person's life and budget, such as saving on insurance rates and large purchases like cars, and that is certainly important. The strategies that I show you in this book can certainly be adapted to help you calculate savings in those areas as well, but the primary focus of this book is showing you how to Calculate Your Savings in your home, particularly in the areas of food and other commonly used household goods. In order to truly benefit from using a frugal strategy, it is critical you know how much the strategy is really benefitting you to determine whether it is worth your investment of time, energy, and possibly money. Bottom line, you must know where you are, and have an idea of where you are going.

For example, it is not unusual for families with young children to purchase 4 or 5 boxes of cereal per month, at about $4 per box. That amounts to $20 per month, or $240 per year for cereal. That price may not look too bad, but it would probably seem high if you knew you could get the same exact boxes of cereal if you purchased them at $2.50 a box when they were on sale, which means $150 for a whole year's worth of cereal ($90 savings). That $240 yearly price for cereal looks even worse once you are aware that you can combine that $2.50 sale price with coupons and rebates and potentially spend under $60 for a whole year's worth of cereal ($180 savings). Implementing these strategies on just 10 to 15 of your most commonly purchases household items will easily save you thousands of dollars over time.

As a mother who works full-time outside of the home, I certainly don't have time to implement every "frugal" tip, but I have found that consistently executing some key frugal strategies pays off extremely well! I wrote this book to help busy people identify which frugal strategies to integrate into their busy lives. This book is not about being a gourmet chef, a professional home-organizer or a coupon "diva", because those things I am not. I am a woman who loves the idea of living frugally, and I have figured out how to determine which strategy to use and when. At various points over the past few years, I've been an avid coupon user, planted a garden, line dried clothes, made baby food, and used various other money-saving strategies in my home. Some of these strategies required a lot of planning and effort, and as I reflect back, I wonder whether my time and effort were worth the savings. In this book, I show you how I am able to calculate the benefits of using any frugal strategy and determine if it is right for me.

The skills I will teach you will allow you to focus on the strategies that are most beneficial for you and your family, in your home today. Seasons change, and so will the frugal strategies that are best for you, so don't get attached to any particular method of saving money. However, frugality can always be practiced in some form and should be implemented into your life no matter what season you are in.

Many people view frugality as a negative, a title to be bestowed upon those who are poor or stingy. I view frugality as a blessing and a way to serve my family by being a good steward of what we have been blessed with. Frugality is a very broad subject. Everything from using the last drop of toothpaste in a tube to saving for a child's college education can be classified as being frugal. In addition, frugality does not look the same in every home: What works well in my home may not work for you. In order for strategies to be successful and sustainable in YOUR home, it is important to learn about a variety of ways to save time and money, and then exercise wisdom in determining which ways can best serve you.

A person who is frugal utilizes his or her time, money and energy efficiently in order to maximize value and productivity in every area of life. Put simply, being frugal means asking, "How can I get the best product or service at the best price and spend the least amount of time and energy doing so?"

Frugality is a balancing act where one must weigh the costs of time, energy and money against the expected outcome. You must determine if the outcome is worth the resources you are investing. Of course, you can spend ten hours on a Saturday driving around town buying one fantastically priced product each at 12 different stores, but is it worth your time and energy? Only you can decide.

How to Assess
a Frugal Strategy

If you want to "assess a frugal strategy" you must take these two basic steps:

1. Compare the cost of a strategy to the benefit of it.
2. Calculate how much you will save.

Only after following these steps will you have a clear picture of the value a frugal strategy can add to your life. These steps require some effort up front, but they will save you from the frustration, wasted time and disappointment that comes from forcing yourself and your family to do something that is difficult to do effectively and not worth the effort.

Throughout this book, I provide several tables to help you calculate your savings and determine the benefits of using specific strategies. The best way to use these tables is to copy them into a notebook or journal that should be used exclusively for tracking your frugal strategies and savings. This notebook you create can become a great resource as you begin or continue on your journey to becoming more frugal.

Cost vs. Benefit

Countless frugal strategies exist, and more often than not they have the potential to add value to your life. However, one can experience "frugal burnout." Do you want to wear yourself out trying to line dry ten loads of laundry a week when you have a crawling ten month old baby (those baby socks are the worst!)? Is the $20 savings on your electric bill worth the two hours per week of your time hanging clothes? Maybe it is for you; only you can decide. Maybe those two hours per week would provide greater benefit to your family if you used them to learn a new skill.

The question you should ask yourself is, *"Which strategies should I use now given my current resources of time, money and energy?"* In order to truly see the benefits of being frugal, you must determine which of the countless tips, tricks, and methods will give you and your family the biggest return on the investment of your resources.

The best strategies are different for every family, and even what works for your family today may not work six months or a year from now. It is very important to constantly assess why you are doing something and whether that something is helping or hurting you. Your needs and the seasons of your life will constantly change, and these tools can help you to determine what best suits your needs at any given point in time.

A quick search of the internet will provide you with countless frugal strategies, and here is a short list of a few I have used:

Kids
Cloth diapers
Make baby food
Borrow toys and books (from a friend, the library, etc.)
Purchase gently used 2nd hand items (toys, books and clothes)
Use free online resources for crafts and games

Food
Buy snacks in bulk and package them yourself
Make your own "convenience" foods and spice mixes
Eat more beans and less meat
Cook at home from scratch
Cook more than one meal at a time and freeze for later
Pack lunches for all members of the family

Home
Use homemade laundry soaps and cleaners
Line dry clothes
Use cloth napkins
Grow a garden
Learn basic sewing skills

General
Use coupons for commonly purchased items
Take advantage of free entertainment (libraries, museum, etc.)
Find free or inexpensive ways to be healthy and stay active

Starting with the end goal in mind is very important. For example, are you trying to save money to go on a nice vacation or to pay off debt? Are you saving up for your children's college education? Knowing the "why" is very powerful motivation, and it helps you to stay focused on the end goal and not the day to day monotony of being frugal.

Calculating the cost of a certain strategy can help you determine whether the strategy is going to be beneficial to your life. To do this, you need to determine the time, money and effort necessary to utilize the strategy and compare it to the benefits, such as financial savings, health/well-being, and time savings that you will reap from using the strategy.

Remember that money is not the only resource worth saving or being mindful of. Some frugal strategies may not save money up front, but instead you may save time or add to your health and well-being. For example, planting a garden will cost you money as well as time and effort up front, and the benefits will not be seen for months to come. You must compare the time and cost of planting it along with the time and effort required to tend to it to the financial and health benefits you will reap at harvest time. Only you and your family can determine whether the cost is worth the benefit, and I will show you how to make that comparison. Continuing with the garden example, as you gain the experience and equipment necessary to plant, harvest and store your produce, the strategy will become easier to implement. The next time you decide to use this strategy, the cost, money, time and effort to plant it will decrease, while the net benefits from tending and harvesting will likely increase.

Evaluating Costs and Benefits
in Different Domains

1. Identify one strategy that you would like to implement. To get started, this strategy can be as general as "use more coupons," or as specific as "create a weekly menu plan for dinner meals."

2. Assign a score to each of the costs (time invested, effort invested and money invested) and benefits (time savings, health & well-being, money savings) of the strategy. Guidelines are shown in the following tables. How this works is that if a cost and/or benefit is positive for you (e.g., the time invested is low or the time saved is high), then it gets a higher score. If the cost/benefit is negative for you (e.g., the money invested is high or the money saved is low), then it gets a lower score. This cost/benefit exercise is meant to give you a quick way to determine if a strategy is worth your consideration. Remember that what may work for you at one point in time will probably not work in the future so it is important to reassess periodically.

Strategy:	
Cost/Benefit	Score (Circle Value for Each Cost/Benefit)
Time Invested	0 / 10 / 20
Effort Invested	0 / 5 / 10
Money Invested	0 / 10 / 20
Time Saved	0 / 10 / 20
Health & Well Being	0 / 5 / 10
Money Saved	0 / 10 / 20
Total:	

Cost: Time Invested	
This is time you will spend actually implementing the strategy, but does not include any shopping required	Score
Low Time: Strategy can be completed in less than 30 minutes per week	20
Medium Time: Strategy requires more than 30 minutes but less than 1 hour per week to complete and requires attention on more than one day per week to implement	10
High Time: Strategy requires more than 1 hour per day to complete and requires your attention on more than 3 days per week	0

Cost: Effort Invested	
This is the level of planning, shopping or other "background" work that must be completed prior to actually implementing the strategy. It is also the level of exertion and how often you must attend to the strategy. A strategy that needs your exclusive and undivided attention would require more effort than one that could be accomplished along with another task.	Score
Low Effort: Strategy would require little to no effort or planning and you can easily implement it without having to rearrange your schedule and without it having an impact on your family, work or social life. This strategy requires no physical exertion and may even work without your physical presence.	10
Medium Effort: Strategy would require some effort and you might have to cancel/reschedule 1-2 events per month in order to effectively implement this strategy.	5
High Effort: Strategy would require you to cancel/reschedule at least one personal, family or social event per week. This strategy might cause you to exert a lot of physical energy and you might need the assistance of others to complete.	0

Cost: Money Invested	
This is the amount of money that is required for you to plan, implement and maintain a strategy over the course of a month	**Score**
Little Money: Implementing this strategy is free, will not cost you more than what you typically spend in a month to accomplish the same task, or will cost you less than 10% more than what you typically spend in a month to accomplish the same task.	20
Medium Money: Implementing this strategy will cost you more than 10% and up to 50% more than what you typically spend in a month to accomplish the same task.	10
High Money: Implementing this strategy will cost you to pay over 50% more than what you typically pay in a month to accomplish the same task.	0

Benefit: Time Savings	
This is time you would save on a daily basis once the strategy is completed	**Score**
Saves Lots: This strategy would save you and/or others 30 minutes to 1 hour or more daily (or as often as it is performed) compared to the time it took prior to having the strategy in place	20
Saves Some: This strategy would save you and/or others 5 - 30 minutes daily (or as often as it is performed) compared to the time it took prior to having the strategy in place	10
Saves Little/Costs Time: This strategy would save less than 5 minutes or may cost some extra time compared to the time it required prior to having the strategy in place.	0

Benefit: Health & Well Being	
This is the impact this strategy will have on your health and wellbeing and that of the others who are impacted by its implementation. This includes the impact the strategy will have on your home environment	Score
Great Impact: This strategy removes opportunities to make poor choices and inspires healthy choices on a DAILY basis. May cause a decrease in stress, decrease in weight, healthier food options, and/or more quality time as a family. For home, less clutter and unused items, more peace and fewer arguments	10
Medium Impact: This strategy has some impact on the health and well-being of you and your family, but its impact is only felt one or two times per week	5
Little/Negative Impact: This strategy has little to no impact on the health and wellbeing of you, your family or your home environment. This could also be something that negatively impacts the health and well being of your family or the peace and order in your home environment.	0

Benefit: Financial Savings	
This is the amount of money you will save after the strategy has been implemented	Score
High Savings: Implementing this strategy will save you over 50% of what you typically spend.	20
Medium Savings: This strategy saves 10% to 50% of what you typically spend to accomplish the same task and/or purchase the same item	10
Little Savings/Costs Money: Implementing this strategy does not save any money and may actually cost you more after implementation	0

Evaluating Your Score

Below 70 - If a strategy scores below 70 points, it will likely require a lot of time, money and/or energy in order to implement and is likely not worthwhile for you.

70—79 - If a strategy scores between 70 and 79 points, you should reconsider the strategy in the future to see if its score changes. Strategies in this range, will not provide the greatest return on your investment of time, money and/or energy under current conditions.

80-100 - If a strategy scores between 80 and 100 points, make plans to start implementing it today! Strategies that score in this range will provide you with the greatest benefits. They are likely easy to do and benefits will outweigh the resources used.

Please remember that scores are unique in every situation. They depend upon on your initial skill level, your schedule, and your budget. You may have grown up in a family that grew vegetables in a garden or on a farm. Now you may live in a large city and hold a 9-5 job. Would it be possible for you to try to implement some of the strategies you were raised with? Would it be beneficial? Issues like these need to be evaluated.

Now, review the preceding list of common frugal strategies (or find your own) and assign a score of 0-100 based upon the "Cost/Benefit" analysis and choose 3-5 strategies that score above 80. Congratulations! You have just found the best strategies for saving money in your home!

In the next section, I detail how you can calculate how much you typically spend on a certain strategy or product and how much you would spend using more frugal means. Comparing these costs will help you clearly see how much you might save.

Example of the Scoring of a Specific Strategy

Strategy: Packing Lunch Rather than Purchasing Fast Food Daily	
Cost/Benefit	Score (Circle Value for Each Cost/Benefit)
Cost: Time Invested	0 / 10 / (20)
Cost: Effort Invested	0 / 5 / (10)
Cost: Money Invested	0 / 10 / (20)
Benefit: Time Saved	0 / 10 / (20)
Benefit: Health & Well-Being	0 / 5 / (10)
Benefit: Money Saved	0 / 10 / (20)
Total:	100

In this example, I compared the costs and benefits of packing a lunch daily. For me, packing a lunch requires little to no extra time and effort; most of the time, I simply pack leftovers from my evening meal into containers so it's ready to go the next day. So I gave "time invested" and "effort invested" the highest scores of 20 and 10 respectively. For someone who does not cook regularly, more time and effort would be required to pack lunch every work day. In this case, the score for "time invested" might be a 10 and the score for "effort invested" might be a 5. Another consideration is that more often than not, the cost of a serving of leftovers or even a homemade sandwich is pennies, so the score for "money invested" in most cases will be a 20. However, if your packed lunch incorporates filet mignon, it will be more expensive than the $5 fast food meal you might normally purchase, so the "money invested" would be high and a score of 0 would be appropriate.

Remember, just like with any frugal strategy, you will need to find balance. I would not advocate that you purchase lunch from a restaurant every day, nor would I advocate that you take your homemade lunch every single day; however, I would suggest you should be aware of your budget and spend accordingly. For example, if you typically spend about $10 per workday on lunch, that equals roughly $200 per month, or $2400 per year. Awareness of your spending is critical. After recognizing that you spend $200 monthly on lunch meals, you may wish to reduce this amount and aim to spend only $100 or $50 per month on lunch meals. By simply being aware of your spending, and intentional about your strategies to save, reducing your monthly spending on lunch to $50 would allow you to intentionally repurpose that $1800 yearly savings.

How to Calculate Your Savings©

Now that you have determined which strategies are best for you and your family, I will detail how to calculate your savings. In order to calculate your savings, it is important that you know what you are currently spending on a product or service so that you can compare it to what your costs would be after adopting the chosen frugal strategy. Calculating your savings works well for specific items and specific tasks that have a start and end date as well as a set budget. For example, it is difficult to truly calculate total savings for something as broad as "using coupons" without first defining the items you will use the coupons for and the timeframe in which you will use up the product.

In a nutshell, these are the steps needed to Calculate Your Savings©:

1. Identify a goal for a specific item, task or service that has a specific start and end date and specific budget.

2. Calculate the amount (daily, weekly, monthly, or yearly) you currently spend on the item, task, or service.

3. Identify two or more "Frugal" alternatives.

4. Calculate the costs of each alternative.

5. Calculate Your Savings© by determining how much less you would spend compared to what you currently spend.

Here is an example. Let's say that finding a more frugal way to wash clothes was one of the strategies that would work best for you and your family, and you currently spend $20 a month on laundry detergent by buying a $5 (non-sale price) bottle of detergent each week. Typically, this bottle washes about 20 loads for your family, so costs you about $0.25 per load. You could start seeing some savings by simply purchasing a larger size that has a lower price per load; if you buy a $15 bottle of detergent that washes 100 loads of laundry, then you would be paying $0.15 per load. That is a savings of 40% just by simply purchasing a larger size. Over the course of a year, you would be spending around $156 for laundry detergent instead of the roughly

$240 it would cost you to purchase $5 bottles.

The savings really start to add up when you strategize to combine sales and coupons and get the detergent for free or nearly free. This could be done by purchasing the $5 bottle when it is on sale for $2.50 and, while also using a coupon when the bottle is at the $2.50 sale price, for example. Another frugal way to wash clothes is to use homemade laundry soap. I've used this strategy personally, and my homemade laundry soap cost me $0.02 per load. An added benefit of using homemade laundry soap is that it allows you to control what is in it and minimize exposure to dyes and other irritants if you have a family member with allergies.

Goal: Save Money on Washing Clothes; Current Cost: $0.25 per Load

Frugal Alternatives	Cost	Savings Over Current Cost
Purchase Larger Size	0.15 per Load	40%
Combine Sales & Coupons	0.00 to 0.10 per Load	60% - 100%
Homemade Laundry Soap	0.02 per Load	92%

Like with every strategy, it is important to have an idea of the amount of time, energy, and money you are willing to put into implementing it. Purchasing a larger size doesn't require extra effort or time, but it does require more money up front and storage space. Combining sales with coupons doesn't require more money, but it does require time and effort in researching and shopping for the best deals. Making your own laundry soap requires time, effort, and money up front, but you can prepare it to last for months at a time and count on sustained savings over time.

Part II:
How "Frugal" Works for Me

My Top Strategies

First of all, let me reiterate that I am a mother of a preschooler, and I work full-time outside of my home. At this point in my life, I simply do not have the time and energy required to implement many frugal strategies in my day to day life. However, I have a very strong desire to create a home that is comfortable, well-stocked with what we need, and a place of refuge. For me, a large part of this comfort and refuge comes in the form of meeting our most basic nutritional, health and personal-care needs. Therefore, the majority of the strategies I use to save time and money are those related to food, my household, and my kitchen. In Part 2 of this book, I share how I have implemented some of these strategies.

There are many ways to be frugal, and again, I would venture to say that in our society NO ONE has time to implement every frugal strategy! However, no matter what stage of life you are in or how busy you are, this book will offer some strategies that will help you get your budget under control!

Of course, the top strategies for you and your family may look completely different than mine, and that is perfectly fine. After you have armed yourself with the tools in Part 1 of this book, you will be the best judge of what will work best for you at the current time. Being frugal is not a one-size fits all tip or trick, and as your family changes, so should your strategies.

Maybe you are a "work-at-home" mother, who manages endless cleaning, feeding, carpooling, nursing, homeschooling, disciplining, entertaining, and counseling. You are literally on call 24-7! During my three months of maternity leave, I quickly learned that staying home did not automatically equate to living life more aware of where money was going. I also realized that even with the best intentions, living a frugal lifestyle is hard to accomplish without a plan, even when you working full-time in the home. It's easy to simply buy the cheapest products, but that is not truly the essence of sustainable frugality.

Maybe you are a single adult who works 60 hours a week and you find yourself in the fast food drive thru lane more than a few times a week. You too can benefit from these tools and figure out how you could best fit frugality into your busy schedule.

For my food and household expenses, the three main areas in which I implement frugal techniques are Planning, Shopping, and Food Preparation. When I calculate my savings, these are the high scoring strategies for me. Under each of these "Big Three," there are many smaller tips and strategies I have used in various ways over the past five years.

Planning
Menu planning
Scheduling
Organizing

Shopping
Learn coupon basics
Know your buy price

Food Preparation:
Learn cooking basics
Bulk cook (preparing multiple meals/snacks at a time)
Make my own convenience foods

For me, Planning, Shopping, and Food Preparation all factor into my goal of saving money on my food budget. I believe that all of the strategies I make use of function together to make it possible for me to accomplish my goal. In the tables below, I show how I determine the cost vs. benefit score for one strategy under each of the three categories (Planning Shopping and Food Preparation). Using these scores, I was able to determine that each of these strategies have benefits that outweigh their costs and work well for my life right now, but you may need to use different strategies.

Strategy: Planning, Dinner Menus	
Cost/Benefit	**Score (Circle Value for Each Cost/Benefit)**
Cost: Time Invested	(0) / 10 / 20
Cost: Effort Invested	0 / 5 / (10)
Cost: Money Invested	0 / 10 / (20)
Benefit: Time Saved	0 / 10 / (20)
Benefit: Health & Well-Being	0 / 5 / (10)
Benefit: Money Saved	0 / 10 / (20)
Total:	80

Strategy: Shopping, Use Coupons for 5-10 Specific Items	
Cost/Benefit	**Score (Circle Value for Each Cost/Benefit)**
Cost: Time Invested	0 / 10 / (20)
Cost: Effort Invested	0 / 5 / (10)
Cost: Money Invested	0 / 10 / (20)
Benefit: Time Saved	0 / 10 / (20)
Benefit: Health & Well-Being	0 / 5 / (10)
Benefit: Money Saved	0 / 10 / (20)
Total:	85

Strategy: Food Preparation, Bulk Cook	
Cost/Benefit	Score (Circle Value for Each Cost/Benefit)
Cost: Time Invested	0 / 10 / (20)
Cost: Effort Invested	0 / 5 / (10)
Cost: Money Invested	0 / 10 / (20)
Benefit: Time Saved	0 / 10 / (20)
Benefit: Health & Well-Being	0 / 5 / (10)
Benefit: Money Saved	0 / 10 / (20)
Total:	85

As you see, one of my current strategies is to use coupons, but only for specific items, not for every single item that I purchase. For me, this particular use of coupons scores 85, and fits well into my life right now. At one point in my life, I was an avid coupon user, and I devoted many hours each week to planning my shopping trips and striving to use coupons for as many items as possible. As shown in the following table, my score for couponing to that extent would be 55. This is why I modified my use of coupons to only use them for a specific number of items, and it makes the strategy much easier for me to implement (as shown in the previous table regarding coupons).

Strategy: Shopping, Use Coupons for as Many Items as Possible	
Cost/Benefit	Score (Circle Value for Each Cost/Benefit)
Cost: Time Invested	(0) / 10 / 20
Cost: Effort Invested	(0) / 5 / 10
Cost: Money Invested	0 / (10) / 20
Benefit: Time Saved	0 / 10 / (20)
Benefit: Health & Well-Being	0 / (5) / 10
Benefit: Money Saved	0 / 10 / (20)
Total:	55

Here's an example: Using the "Calculate Your Savings©" technique detailed in Part I, I show the cost savings I could see for the goal of Saving Money on Dinner. The same format applies for similar goals, such as Saving Money on Weekday Lunch or Saving Money on Cleaning Products. In order to successfully accomplish your goals, you have to determine which goals and timelines will work best for you at this point in your life.

For the following example, I compare the price of an average dinner at a restaurant to the price of a couple of alternatives.

Goal: Save Money on Monthly Dinner

Current Cost: Average Monthly Restaurant Cost for Dinner Meals per Person = $240 ($8.00 per meal)

Frugal Alternatives	Cost per Month	Savings Over Current Cost
Purchase Cheaper Take Out ($3.00 per meal)	$90.00	63%
Create Monthly Dinner Menu Plan and Budget ($2.00 per meal)	$60.00	75%

This cost breakdown shows why I have chosen to focus on my household and food expenses with my frugality. With a goal of saving money on meals, one can easily save over 75% by preparing healthy meals at home.

The remainder of Part II details how I have actually implemented some of these strategies with my food and household expenses. In this section, I share some ideas for the beginner who hasn't turned on the stove in months and needs some basic steps to begin. I also share some ideas for the intermediate cook who has decent cooking skills but lacks some of the staples needed for cooking complete meals and may also lack organization. Last, I share some ideas for the more advanced cook who has what is needed to prepare meals, but needs more order and planning. The point is that no matter where you fall in the spectrum, striving for more organization and having a plan for your meals and household tasks will lead to great benefits for you and your family.

Under each of the "Big Three" that I outline above - Planning, Shopping and Food Preparation - there are many smaller tips and strategies I have used in various degrees over the past five years. Before discussing the Big Three, I outline a plan for the organization needed to implement them.

Organizing and Cleaning

Organizing a system is absolutely essential in order to be frugal. When your food and household items are organized, you can quickly take inventory of what you have and plan accordingly. You also lower the possibility of having multiples of the same items that are prone to spoiling, which is a complete waste of money.

If you are organized you can develop a stockpile of food and household goods. When your refrigerator, pantry and cabinets are ordered and clean, you can easily buy items at their cheapest price and stockpile them, while being mindful of when you must use them. If those areas are not organized, your home is prone to clutter and wastefulness. Contrary to popular belief, your stockpile does not have to take over your entire basement or garage. If you find stockpiling to be an effective frugal strategy for you, you can stockpile just a few of your family's most commonly used products and still see hundreds or thousands of dollars in savings per year.

Having a system for cleaning your home, specifically your kitchen, goes a long way in being more efficient and saving money. I've found that it is much easier to find the motivation to cook a meal when my kitchen and cookware are clean and ready for use. A common strategy I use is to throw or give away 10 items from my home every day (this applies not only to food items, but other household goods such as toiletries, clothes and toys). This mindset helps me to minimize clutter.

Another helpful tip is to organize your cooking space and cookware. Place commonly used spices and oils near your stove so you can quickly access them when you are cooking and keep an eye on what you need to restock. Have an easily accessible list for quickly jotting down items you are low on. This can be a piece of paper, a whiteboard, or even an app on your phone. Simply writing things down when you first become aware of the need is important in staying organized. Now on to the Big Three.

Planning

A commonly used wise saying is "begin with the end in mind." Nothing will hold more true to someone who is sincerely dedicated to living life more frugally. As you begin or continue on your journey, it is essential that you have a plan. A plan can not only be a source of structure and direction, it can be a source of motivation when the whole idea of being frugal becomes overwhelming. The good things about a plan are that it puts you in control, allows you to see how you could change course, and can be tailored to you and your family. Your plan will guide you in how to best suit your needs and not simply have you going along with the status quo.

Menu Planning: In the arena of food and meals, a menu plan is the best way to develop a road map for success. Menu Planning allows you to be very efficient with your time, energy and money, and this is why it is one of my top frugal strategies. Before buying food or cooking meals, it is always best to have a menu plan. You may start off with a rough plan, but the key is to just start writing things down. You can always add more details once you get the hang of it. Menu plans are most effective when they are weekly or monthly because that allows you to plan ahead and efficiently use or freeze products before they expire. Monthly menu plans are optimal because they allow you to plan for weeks ahead, use bulk cooking techniques, and stock up on products when they are on sale well in advance of when you will actually need them.

For example, let's say that you are starting to contemplate February's menu plan during the last week of January. While shopping, you notice that your store has ground beef on sale for $0.89 per pound. Your family typically eats 2 pounds of ground beef per week, and you normally pay $2.39 per pound. At $2.39 per pound, your monthly cost adds up to $19.12. If you purchase all of the ground beef that your family will need for February during the sale in January, you will pay a total of $7.12, which is a savings of $12.00 (about 65%). Of course, you cannot purchase this perishable product and just let it sit in your fridge for weeks, and that is where bulk cooking becomes important. Of course, you can simply freeze all of the ground beef immediately after you purchase it, and thaw it out as necessary. However, for this product bulk cooking is phenomenal because it helps eliminate some steps in meal preparation during your most hectic times, thereby minimizing the likelihood of you buying unplanned take-out food.

If you are not familiar with bulk cooking (also known as freezer cooking) and how it relates to menu planning, it is a method that calls for you to use your down time (a weekend, for example) to cook large portions of a meal or an entire meal, cool it down, portion it out, and freeze the individual portions until you need them. Every meal cannot be pre-cooked and frozen in this way, but a quick internet search will lead you to hundreds of balanced healthy meals that can be cooked in bulk. Bulk cooking is really helpful, and, for me, it goes hand in hand with menu planning. As you work on mastering the art of creating a monthly menu, bulk cooking can make your days and meal times run much more smoothly.

Another important benefit of menu planning is that it allows you to be efficient with every aspect of your meals. Essentially, planning menus allows you to maximize the use of all ingredients so that nothing gets wasted. If a certain item is perishable, but not freezable, you can plan to cook more than one recipe that calls for it before it goes bad. Alternatively, if a certain item is perishable and freezable, you can use what you need that week and freeze the rest. For example, if a recipe calls for only 1/4 of a cup of chopped onion, chop the entire onion! Put the amount that you will need within the next few days in the refrigerator and the rest in the freezer. The next time you need chopped onions, you won't have to go buy another one or spend any more time chopping. If you are not sure which items are freezable, you can find a wealth of information on the subject by doing a quick internet search.

A menu plan can be as simple as a week's worth of dinners, or as complex as a month's worth of breakfasts, lunches, dinners, and snacks. Depending on the size and preferences of your family, you can use leftovers to limit the number of times you cook during the week while still serving delicious homemade meals. The key to successful menu planning is planning not only your meals but also factoring in the time and energy you will need to prepare them. I provide a sample weekly menu and task list as guidelines for getting started. You can plan to do tasks that require lots of time on days when you are less busy. Additionally, it is helpful to plan what tasks you need to do each day in preparation for the following day or later in the week.

Sample Weekly Lunch and Dinner Menu

	Sunday	Monday	Tuesday
Lunch	Breakfast Foods (waffles, pancakes, omelettes)	Chicken Enchiladas	Leftovers: Grilled Tilapia, Rice & Steamed Veggies
Dinner	Shredded Chicken Enchiladas & Salad	Grilled Tilapia, Rice & Steamed Veggies	Spaghetti, Garlic Bread & Salad

Wednesday	Thursday	Friday	Saturday
Turkey Sandwiches	Turkey Sandwiches	Leftovers: Pot Roast, Potatoes, Green Beans	Turkey Burgers and French Fries
Spaghetti, Garlic Bread & Broccoli	Pot Roast, Potatoes, Green Beans	Turkey Burgers and French Fries	Order Take Out

Sample Weekly Task List for Preparing Dinner

	Sunday	Monday	Tuesday
Tasks	Cook Chicken Enchiladas Prepare Salad Cook Rice for Monday's dinner and Tuesday's Lunch Place Frozen Tilapia in Refrigerator	Season and Cook Tilapia Steam Veggies Warm up Rice Place the Ground Meat for Tuesday's Spaghetti, in Fridge	Cook Meat for Spaghetti Boil pasta for Spaghetti Cook Garlic Bread Assemble Salad
Dinner	Shredded Chicken Enchiladas & Salad	Grilled Tilapia, Rice & Steamed Veggies	Spaghetti, Garlic Bread & Salad

Wednesday	Thursday	Friday	Saturday
Season Roast for Thursday, and leave in Fridge overnight to marinate	Chop, Season and Cook Potatoes Steam Green Beans Place Roast in Pan and Cook Make sure you have Buns, and condiments for burgers	Season and Cook Burgers Cook French Fries	
Spaghetti, Garlic Bread & Broccoli	Pot Roast, Potatoes, Green Beans	Turkey Burgers and French Fries	Order Take Out

Another key to successful menu planning is consolidating steps. It is absolutely critical that you are constantly analyzing your system and asking yourself "How can I be more efficient?" For example, in this sample menu, the protein sources are chicken, tilapia, ground turkey and pot roast. The chicken, ground turkey and pot roast could all be prepared on Sunday evening, if that is when you have time, and stored in the freezer or fridge until needed later that week. Additionally, other parts of the meal can be prepped in advance as well. Let's say that three of your recipes this week call for chopped peppers. Chop all the peppers you will need for the upcoming week on Sunday evening and store in the fridge. You could also place many of the ingredients for the two salads for the week in separate containers so that they are ready to grab when needed. This technique requires that you are mindful of how soon your items may spoil, and an internet search can quickly provide you with this information.

I typically take a large salad for my lunch, and, most of the time I prepare two days' worth of salad, which cuts down on the time I spend prepping lunches overall. I do this by mindfully combining the more hearty items (spinach, carrots, peppers) days in advance, and waiting until the day I will eat the salad to add the items that tend to go bad more quickly over time (eggs, tomatoes, seeds, mushrooms). Of course, there are many variations to this strategy, and the key is to be mindful and aware of the foods you are buying and their shelf-life.

Shopping

After you have planned your menu and written your list, it is time to shop! Ideally, it is best to create or adjust your menu to correlate with what items are on sale. In many cases, you can easily access a store's sales ad on their website. Eventually, you may choose to assemble a stockpile of items that were purchased at the lowest prices, and you can create your menu plan based on items you have in your stockpile.

Learn Coupon Basics: If you are a beginner, couponing requires a significant amount of time to learn how it works, but it can potentially save thousands of dollars a year. There are many free and low cost sites online that can help you get started. Prior to becoming a parent, I used coupons avidly, and I was able to save well over a thousand dollars over the course of a year on many household products including frozen vegetables, toilet tissue, razors, and deodorant. I was even able to get many items for free, and I loved it!

However, I did find that there were some drawbacks to using coupons. For example, many readily available coupons are for convenience foods that are not the healthiest option. Coupons for healthy items like fresh produce are extremely rare. So using coupons may encourage the purchase of unneeded items. Also, I found that in order to see large savings with coupons over time, I needed to spend time researching, planning and shopping around for the best deals. As my schedule became more restricted, this time commitment became a deterrent to me.

Many manufacturers' coupons are readily available online and in local newspapers, and some stores have their own coupons (which can only be used at the given store). The best way to use coupons is to combine the manufacturer's coupon with the store coupons on an item that is on sale. Many items can be obtained for free or nearly free by using this strategy, although some stores do not allow the combination of coupons. This is one area where your commitment to researching coupon use will be required. Knowledge of your local stores' coupon policies is critical to effectively using coupons, and be aware that policies may change over time.

There are countless websites and resources that can teach all of the basic skills required to efficiently use coupons, and I will leave that task to them. However, as a once devoted coupon user, I can say that if your schedule and life situation allows for you to spend hours researching, clipping and shopping, it can definitely be worth the effort.

Know Buy Prices: Identifying the "Buy Price" of an item is critical to saving on your food budget. The Buy Price is what you consider to be the lowest price for an item you're going to find, and it is the price at which you buy enough of it to last until it goes on sale at this price again. For many items, this means finding the item on sale and using a coupon or two during your purchase. By purchasing certain items at their Buy Price and using coupons, I have been able to get toothpaste, toothbrushes, razors, frozen vegetables, condiments, soap, toilet tissue, shampoo and various other household items for up to 90% off or even FREE! For example, while I was stockpiling diapers during my pregnancy, my Buy Price was $0.10 per diaper. Diapers are normally $0.20 - $0.40 a piece when they are not on sale, so this was a savings of up to 75%. Keep in mind that the "buy price" for your favorite brand may not be the lowest for that particular product, especially if you are brand loyal; however, you can still save hundreds of dollars by buying on sale and using coupons, especially on diapers and other items that quickly eat up your budget.

Examples of Potential Savings

Item	Yearly Quantity	Non-Sale Price	Non-Sale Price Per Year (total)	Buy Price	Buy Price Per Year (total)	Non-Sale Price – Buy Price (Per Year)
Ketchup	5 bottles	$2.99	$14.95	$0.00	$0.00	$14.95
Chicken Breasts	80 pounds	$4.99	$399.20	$1.99	$159.20	$240.00
Ground Turkey	96 pounds	$4.95	$475.20	$1.99	$191.04	$284.16
Strawberries	24 pints	$3.99	$95.76	$1.50	$36.00	$59.76
Butter	10 pounds	$3.99	$39.90	$1.00	$10.00	$29.90
Toilet Tissue	6 packages	$11.99	$71.94	$5.00	$30.00	$41.94
Dishwashing Liquid	10 bottles	$1.99	$19.90	$0.00	$0.00	$19.90
Soap	50 bars	$1.25	$62.50	$0.66	$33.33	$29.17
Toothpaste	10 tubes	$3.99	$39.90	$0.00	$0.00	$39.90
Diapers	2250	$0.40	$900.00	$0.10	$225.00	$675.00
Totals			**$2,119.25**		**$684.57**	**$1,434.68**

This table shows how you can save well over $1000 a year by buying just 10 items at their Buy Price. Imagine the saving you will have when you shop for 20 or 30 of your most commonly purchased items this way.

It is extremely time-consuming to follow and track buy prices for every store and for every product that your family uses. However, if you can identify the top 5 or 10 most frequently purchased items for your family and identify their buy price, over time you will start to see significant savings. The table is a sample breakdown for my family of two. Depending on the size of your family, your savings on just one item could be hundreds, if not thousands. For example, let's say that your family of five typically consumes 80 pounds of chicken breasts in a year. If you are able to purchase all of that chicken at $1.99 per pound, you will pay $159 versus nearly $400 at the $4.99 per pound price.

Here are lists of a few basic commonly used household and food items that comprise the bulk of many families' budgets. Every family is different, so tailoring the list to your needs will be necessary.

Household Items
Toilet Tissue
Soap
Deodorant
Dishwashing Liquid
Diapers
Toothpaste
Razors
Feminine Hygiene Products
Pet Food
Over The Counter Medication

Food
Ground meats
Chicken
Beef
Milk
Eggs
Bread
Cereal
Snacks (Chips/Cookies)
Ice Cream
Fruits/Vegetables

As you are trying to identify the Buy Price for an item, whenever possible, try not to be brand or store loyal because it takes more time and that loyalty may dampen your savings. Once you identify the Buy Price for an item and the item is at that price, that is the time you purchase as many as you can and stockpile. If an item is perishable, buy only as much as you will be able to use up before the next time the item will be at this price. If you make a mistake and buy too much of something, a good way to keep it from being wasted is to donate it to another family or a charitable organization.

About brand loyalty: If you think a specific brand is better for you (better tasting or healthier) or if you are health conscious or have dietary restrictions that limit what you can purchase, you can still determine the Buy Price even for these items. Ideally, you are seeking to buy items at their rock-bottom prices, no matter the brand. For example, my family uses a particular brand of soap which is normally $7.50 for 6 bars. I stockpile this soap when its price drops to my $4.00 Buy Price, which saves around 30%. Even though I could probably obtain other brands of soap for free using the Buy Price and coupon strategies, I still purchase this more expensive item at its Buy Price because my family prefers it. Know what works for your family!

In essence, knowing your Buy Price is really about looking at the big picture for the long-term and not just thinking in the moment. It's about slowing down and keeping your eyes open. Yes, of course you could run to your corner drugstore and purchase a bottle of ketchup for $2.99 because burgers are on the menu tonight and you forgot to add it to your shopping list last week. It's only $2.99, so it's no big deal...right? Maybe $2.99 is not a big deal, but it may be the case that the same exact bottle of ketchup is on sale for $1.00 at your local grocery store, and there is a manufacturer's coupon in the newspaper for $0.50 that your grocery store would double to $1.00. This scenario would make the bottle of ketchup absolutely free (barring the price of the newspaper), and with multiple coupons, you might have been able to stockpile enough ketchup to last for a year at essentially no cost. So, no, $2.99 is no big deal, but if you have a habit of purchasing items on a whim, you are paying a premium, and the costs do add up! If you spend $20 on unplanned items every week, the cost adds up to over $1000 per year. If other members of your family have the same habit, you can see how very quickly those extra costs can add up to the cost a trip to somewhere warm and tropical. The ketchup example is one small scenario, but the same principle applies to more expensive items on your shopping list.

Stockpiling

Stockpiling is the process of purchasing multiples of an item and storing them for future use. You can stockpile practically anything, but stockpiling works best for items that are nonperishable or items that can be frozen. To create an efficient stockpile you must purchase at its Buy Price as many of an item as you can store and that you will use before it expires. Stockpiles can have many items or just a few, but awareness is critical.

At this phase in my life, I stockpile only a few key items. I have not found stockpiling every item my family needs to be the best strategy for me at this time because a massive stockpile requires a large commitment of time to create and maintain. However, the items I choose to purchase in bulk are typically those that have a long shelf-life and/or those that my family uses a lot. I generally have 5 to 10 items that we use regularly and that I track the buy prices for, including toilet tissue, toothpaste, eggs, soap, oatmeal and chicken.

Food Preparation

Food preparation is the key to saving on your food budget and also to providing healthier options for your family.

Learn Cooking Basics: A few basic food prep skills are necessary for you to start saving. In our fast paced society, it is important to have the skills to prepare at least a few basic balanced meals for yourself and your family. Even if you are not at a point where you want to start planning monthly or weekly menus, you can still save money if you can identify 5 - 10 meals that can be prepared quickly, and you keep the supplies for those meals on hand.

The internet is jam packed with websites and videos with step by step instructions on how to cook hamburgers, filet mignon and everything in between. The key to learning to cook is simply to begin. I am no gourmet chef, but it is very important to me that my family eats healthy, nutritious and tasty meals at home most of the time. Just like with any skill in life, cooking is learned by doing, and it is a skill that will easily save you thousands of dollars. Most importantly, cooking can be very beneficial to the overall health and well-being of your family.

Bulk Cook: Bulk cooking entails preparing double or even triple portions of a meal and storing the portions that are not going to been eaten immediately in the refrigerator or freezer. This strategy is used by those who are very advanced and dedicated to saving money. In order to be used most effectively, this strategy requires that you have the funds in your budget to purchase food that you and your family may not eat for weeks or months, and that you have the freezer space to store this food. This strategy also requires a lot of planning and organization to ensure that the ingredients are used before spoiling or expiring.

I've seen examples where an entire monthly menu for a family was cooked and stored in the fridge and freezer in one day. Bulk cooking is multi-tasking at its finest. I, however, have done bulk cooking on a much smaller scale, but I still find it to be a great time saver. For example, often when I cook a meal which uses ground meat, I season and cook twice as much as I need and freeze half. The next time I prepare a recipe that calls for ground meat, I can thaw it overnight and have a head start on the meal for the next evening. This has been a huge time saver and has also made it more likely that I will cook on those evenings when I feel less than inspired.

Another much smaller aspect of "bulk cooking" is to prepare some aspects of a meal beforehand. For example, if your family eats six hard-boiled eggs over the course of three days, save time by boiling all of the eggs while you are preparing another meal. Sources indicate the eggs will be good for a week in the shell in the refrigerator.

If you are planning on cooking in bulk, always look for ways to be more efficient by asking questions like "What can be baking in the oven while I am cooking on the stovetop?" or "What snacks can I portion out while I am waiting for a meal to finish cooking?"

Make Your Own Convenience Foods: Convenience food can be an alternative when you are short on time, and you can comfortably fit them in your budget. However, if you are having a hard time getting your food budget to last for the month, this may be an area in which you can reap some huge savings.

One type of "convenience" food are foods or drinks designed for quick and easy consumption, and often pre-packaged in individual serving sizes. These items include, but are not limited to crackers, soft drinks, cookies, juice boxes, bottled water, flavored oatmeal packets, granola bars, pre-cut fruit or vegetables, frozen waffles, candy, baby food, cake mixes, boxed meals, single-serving sized yogurt, frozen dinners and snacks like potato chips; in truth, the list is almost endless! Not only are most of these foods laden with calories, additives, salts and preservatives that aren't good for us, most are very expensive when compared to their "inconvenient" counterparts. The checkout line of most grocery stores is stocked to the brim with many of these "convenience" foods and drinks. This item placement is designed to get consumers to purchase these items on impulse. These items are often 2-3 times more expensive than the exact same item elsewhere in the store at a lower price per unit. However, those managing the product placement have long realized that once a customer is in line and sees a bag of candy she wants, she is much more likely to grab the "convenient" bag at the checkout than she is to leave her place in line and go find the larger sized item at a lower price per unit.

Convenience foods are not always a bad thing, but the cost of these items can quickly add up. If you are trying to save on your food budget, it is important for you to calculate how much you spend on these items, and how much you could save if you portioned some of them at home. Another benefit is that you can tailor make your snacks based on what you like and your health needs.

Another type of convenience food is packaged food you could make yourself. This includes things like oatmeal packets, granola bars, cookies, muffins, and popcorn. Also, boxed meal starters like macaroni and cheese are convenience items. Although these items are often very cheap, they are often very unhealthy and a homemade version of the product would be even cheaper and healthier. Making homemade convenience items is a great way to save in your budget and provide healthier food for you and your family.

Here are a few examples comparing the prices of convenient single serving items to their more frugal counterparts.

Item: Cookies

Option	Total Amount	Product Description	Cost	Cost Per 1.25 ounce Serving	Yearly Cost for 260 Servings
1	2.5 ounces	Package of 2 Large Cookies	$0.99	$0.49	$128.70
2	82.5 ounces	Bulk Package of 66 Large Cookies	$21.99	$0.33	$85.80
3	25 ounces	Homemade Batch of 20 Large Cookies	$3.00	$0.15	$39.00

In the cookie comparison, it is observed that option #3 provides the largest savings, with a yearly savings of almost $90 over option #1.

Item: Iced Tea

Option	Total Amount	Product Description	Cost	Cost Per 23.5 ounce Serving	Yearly Cost for 260 Servings
1	23.5 ounces	1 Individual Can of Sweetened Tea	$0.99	$0.99	$257.40
2	128 ounces	1 Gallon Jug of Sweetened Tea	$5.00	$0.91	$238.67
3	128 ounces	Homemade Tea made of 1 cup of sugar, 6 tea bags and 1 gallon of water	$0.42	$0.08	$20.05

In the iced tea comparison, it is observed that option # 3 provides the largest savings, with a nearly $230 yearly savings over option #1. Both the cookie and iced tea comparisons show the difference in prices between the convenient single serving product, the larger package and the homemade product. For some, a savings of $90 to $230 may not be worth the effort required to make more convenience items at home. However, when you consider that multiple members of your family may be purchasing multiple items at their most expensive prices, you can see how these costs may quickly add up. As you can see from these examples, portioning out bulk items, and preparing homemade snacks, drinks and other convenience products are excellent ways to save money.

I have used the strategy of making my own convenience items in many ways over the past few years. Most notably, I made most of my son's baby food by steaming and pureeing organic vegetables and freezing it in portions. This greatly reduced my need to purchase those little jars of baby food, which I consider to be a convenience item. My primary reason in doing this was because I perceive it to be healthier than the standard baby food available on the market. Not only was this strategy much cheaper and healthier than the convenient baby food, an added bonus to making his food was that his palate was trained to like fresh vegetables without any added preservatives, salts or fillers. Now, as a preschooler, he will eat a plateful of vegetables without any protest. Unlike many children his age, he actually loves fresh vegetables! For the few months that he ate baby food, he was served purchased baby food only if we were away from home for an extended period of time; I even sent homemade baby food with him for lunch at daycare. For the most part, besides breast milk and baby cereal, his diet consisted of steamed and pureed organic foods (vegetables, fruits and later meats) that I prepared in my home.

Here is an excerpt adapted from my journal written when my son was 7 months old:

"My adventure into "organic homemade baby food" is turning out to be VERY rewarding. I made a batch of sweet potato puree last Friday and he has been loving it! One of his teachers at daycare commented that it smells so much better than the jarred stuff. Here's the break-down: I paid $2.98 for a 3 pound bag of organic sweet potatoes. From that, I made about 45 ounces of puree, which equals about $0.06 per ounce. Organic jarred sweet potato (plus preservatives, eww!) is about $0.26 per ounce. So that is a savings of over 75%, and most important-ly it is much healthier. WIN, WIN, WIN!!!!"

As I reflect, I believe that my son's first year of life was the beginning of my quest to combine frugality and efficiency with the desire to add to the health and well-being of myself and my family. What this re-quires is a keen awareness of what my family and I need, and the disci-pline to research the best ways to meet those needs. You will find that as you remove or eliminate much of the "convenience," you will have to spend more time and energy doing the actual work. At this season of my life, when I calculate my savings, it's well worth it.

My commitment to breastfeeding my son for a year (breast milk is the ultimate convenience food!), and preparing homemade baby food was not at all based on my desire to save money, it was based upon my de-sire to simply provide him with the best nutritional start I possibly could. Any and every other benefit, including financial savings, were simply "icing" on the proverbial cake.

During my son's first year of life, I spent $0 on milk formula, probably less than $75 on his homemade pureed foods, plus an additional $125 on baby snacks, cereals and jarred foods for the few times it was used. Yes, that would be a grand total of $200 for feeding a baby from birth through his "baby food" phase, and he received the absolute best nu-trition. During the last few months of his first year, he began to eat more and more table foods, and this cost is not reflected in the $200 figure. Only now, as I reflect upon that time, am I able to see the fi-nancial benefits of my choosing to focus on the health and well-being of my son. I understand that some women are not able to breastfeed, but in addition to homemade baby food, there are a countless number of other strategies to save on expenses for kids. The key is not simply trying to save money, but looking for ways to add to the health and well-being of your family, WHILE saving money.

Four Easy Tips to Help You
Get You Started TODAY

In today's society, there are many misconceptions about frugality. Unfortunately, many people think that living a frugal lifestyle requires a person to be cheap, hungry, and wear worn out clothes! I believe this could not be further from the truth. In my life, frugality has allowed me to focus to pay off debts and save money.

TIP #1 Be Strategic!

In today's fast-paced world of constant connectivity and never-ending to-do lists, very few people have the time or energy to carry out every frugal tip known to man. The key to making a huge positive impact in your home and on your wallet is to be strategic!!! If you are just starting out, look for five to ten ways you can start saving money or time, and put them into practice. Compare the cost to the benefit of each of your proposed strategies as described in Part I, and if it scores higher that 80, implement it! Know your limitations, but also be open to challenging them!

TIP #2 Invest Time Up-front

After you have identified the five to ten best frugal strategies for you, some time is required to make them work. In order to have an accurate picture of how much you are truly saving, you must Calculate Your Savings© by investing time into comparing what you currently pay for the item or service to two or more frugal alternatives (as detailed in Part I of this book). Additionally, some of the strategies you can implement in your home require significant time investments, while others may require very little time. For example, effectively using coupons for most items can require an extreme time investment up-front, but has the potential to save thousands of dollars a year. Another strategy is making baby food at home; it does not require a huge time investment and not only can potentially save hundreds of dollars, it is healthy for your baby!

TIP#3 Tailor to Your Time, Energy and Family Life

Frugality is not "one size fits all" and no two families have the same needs, wants and schedules. You should look to implement the strategies that will influence and affect your family positively. Strategies that require loads of time on an ongoing basis may not be the best for you to implement during certain seasons of life. As a working mom, I've found that investing my time to plan and cook most of our meals provides the best return to our budget AND our health. Therefore, at this season of my life, my time and energy is invested into these key strategies.

Tip #4 Break Frugal Strategies Down into Quick and Easy Tasks

If you only have thirty minutes a day to dedicate to implementing or executing a certain strategy, use that time wisely. Ideally, frugality should make your life easier, not more complicated. Frugality is not about creating a plan and having it executed 8 hours from now; ideally, it's about identifying some quick and easy tasks you can accomplish in little to no time without missing a beat! Ultimately, you should be able to integrate one or a few of these tasks into you day without loads of extra thought or effort. As you work through these tasks consistently and at your own pace, you will be well on your way to a more frugal life!

Get Started NOW!

A lot of money is wasted when we don't want to eat the food we already have, and when we allow the food we have to spoil before we use it. If this sounds like you, these quick tasks will help tackle both of these problems.

The first step in living a more frugal lifestyle is to do an honest evaluation of your family's spending. You must be aware of your present status. Next, it is important you have some idea of where you would like to be, or what you would like to do differently. Would you like to start using coupons? Would you like to cut your food budget by $50 a week? Would you like to cook more? Would you like to serve healthier meals? Take a look at the three levels below and determine which one you can best utilize. Lists will give you a good idea of where you can begin; as you progress through one level, you can add to your skill set by performing the tasks in the next level and also creating your own.

The following sections list simple tasks that you can begin today to start planning for, shopping for and prepping your meals. Each of the tasks listed under the "Basic" section require less than 5 minutes to complete, and each section provides some ideas on how to get started.

Level 1: Setting the Stage

Start here if you haven't turned your stove on in months, you usually eat take out most nights, and you have little or no resources on hand to prepare a meal. Time required for each task is less than five minutes. Most of the kitchen essentials listed here can be purchased at a very reasonable price.

Discard any spoiled or expired food.

Search for 3 or 4 easy dinner recipes you would like to try.

Make sure you have these kitchen essentials to get started: Dish Soap, Cleaning Products, Cleaning Supplies, Dish Towels, Aluminum Foil, Plastic Storage Bags, Plastic Wrap, Lunch Bags and Ice Packs, Pots & Pans, Water Filtering System, Reusable bottles for holding water, coffee, tea, and other beverages to take on the go

Pick up the weekly sales ad from your local stores (or check them online).

Place a small whiteboard in your kitchen. These can be purchased for a small price wherever office supplies are sold if you don't already have one. Use it to jot down items to add to your grocery list and/or to list your weekly menu.

Watch a video on cooking basics.

Create a simple dinner menu for the next week based on what is on sale this week.

Level 1 does not require any actual food shopping; you are simply LAYING THE GROUNDWORK and CREATING A PLAN. You have completed level one when you have some meal ideas and the basic kitchen tools.

Level 2: Getting to Work

You have some food staples on hand, but you are not organized enough to make a balanced meal out of them. You cook dinner once or twice a week most weeks.

Check your inventory, and also clean and organize refrigerator and pantry. Make sure to have these basic items on hand (of course tailor this list to fit the needs of your family); if not, add to shopping list:

Protein: chicken, beef, turkey, beans

Vegetables

Fruit

Dairy: Cheese, Milk, Eggs

Grains: Rice, Flour, Pasta, Bread, Oatmeal

Spices/Seasoning: Salt, Pepper, Seasoning Salt, Garlic Powder, Onion Powder, Chicken & Beef Bouillon Cubes, Parsley, Oregano, Thyme, etc.

Condiments: Soy Sauce, Spaghetti Sauce, Ketchup, Mustard, Cooking Oil etc.

Plan a dinner menu for the following week. These meals can be as simple or advanced as you and your family would like. The point is to get into the habit of planning and shopping for your meals.

Search for 5 new recipes you can add to your menu plan.

Organize your cooking station so that cooking utensils, spices and oils are nearby.

Take a shopping trip based on your inventory needs and menu.

Level 2 requires that you start planning meals and shopping. You are building upon the groundwork laid during level 1. You are ready to move to level 3 once you have consistent nightly dinner meals 4-5 times per week, and you are ready to incorporate more meals and snacks into your menu plan.

Level 3: Advanced

You have a well stocked kitchen and most of the tools you need, but often find yourself throwing out food that goes bad. You cook at home more than three times per week, but you just need a plan and some organization in order to truly reach your savings potential.

Create a breakfast menu and a lunch menu and incorporate leftovers where appropriate.

Chop up and freeze any "freezer friendly" ripe fruit or vegetables that are close to spoiling.

Pack lunch for tomorrow from today's leftovers.

Cook a large pot of dry beans (use in salads, as a side dish or meat alternative).

Make homemade "convenience" foods readily available to minimize impulse purchases (i.e. baby food, trail mix, oatmeal packs, cookies, hard-boiled eggs, etc.).

Continue to add new recipes to your menu plans.

After you have mastered Level 3, you are ready to incorporate some even more advanced skills like monthly bulk cooking and stockpiling.

Thank you for reading this book, and I am confident that you now have more tools that will help you to have more awareness on your frugal journey. Your awareness of where you are today, and where you hope to be tomorrow should provide you with both motivation and guidance. This journey is not about being perfect, it is about striving each day to be intentional with your spending, and getting back on course if you get off track.

For more information, please contact the author at calculateyoursavings365@gmail.com

Appendix

The following tables are included to help you calculate your savings and determine benefits. The best way to use these tables is to get a notebook or journal, re-create the tables inside, and fill out the tables as you see fit, as often as you see fit. The notebook you create can become a great resource as you begin or continue on your journey to becoming more frugal.

Cost vs. Benefit

Calculate Your Savings

Menu Plan

Task List

Buy Price versus Non-Sale Price

Meal Price

Cost Vs. Benefit Table

Instructions:

1. Identify a frugal strategy you are considering

2. Use the following tables to identify a score for the "Time Invested," "Effort Invested," and "Money Invested," "Time Saved," "Health & Well Being," and "Money Saved."

3. Calculate your score.

4. A score of 80 and above indicates that the strategy would greatly benefit you and you should begin it immediately. A score below 80 indicates that the strategy would be challenging for you to employ at this time but you may reconsider at another time in your life.

Time Invested		Effort Invested		Money Invested	
Low Time	20	Low Effort	10	Low Time	20
Medium Time	10	Medium Effort	5	Medium Time	10
High Time	0	High Effort	0	High Time	0

Time Saved		Health/ Well Being		Money Saved	
Saves a Lots	20	High Impact	10	High Savings	20
Saves Some	10	Medium Impact	5	Medium Savings	10
Saves Little/Costs Time	0	Little/Negative Impact	0	Little Savings/Costs Money	0

Strategy:	
Cost/Benefit	**Score (Circle Value for Each Cost/Benefit)**
Cost: Time Invested	0 / 10 / 20
Cost: Effort Invested	0 / 5 / 10
Cost: Money Invested	0 / 10 / 20
Benefit: Time Saved	0 / 10 / 20
Benefit: Health & Well-Being	0 / 5 / 10
Benefit: Money Saved	0 / 10 / 20
Total:	

Calculate Your Savings

Instructions:

1. Identify a goal for a specific item, task or service that has specific start and end dates and budget.

2. Calculate the monthly (or weekly, or yearly) cost of what you currently spend on the item, task, or service.

3. Identify at least 2 "Frugal" alternatives

4. Calculate the costs of each alternative

5. Calculate Your Savings© by determining how much less you would spend compared to what you currently spend.

Goal:

Current Cost:

Frugal Alternatives	Cost	Savings Over Current Cost

Menu Plan

Instructions:

Menu planning can be as simple as your dinner menu, or as complicated as all three meals plus snacks each day. The menu plan is the roadmap to successfully saving money on food expenses. The lack of a plan inevitably leads to impulsive, expensive and often unhealthy meal purchases. Your menu plan gives you more control of what you and your family eat, and it allows you to plan ahead for busy times of the month. An easy way to plan your monthly menu is by using a calendar that is solely for your menu plan and posting it in your kitchen.

	Sun- day	Mon- day	Tues- day	Wednes- day	Thurs- day	Fri- day	Satur- day
Break- fast							
Lunch							
Dinner							
Snacks							

	Sunday	Monday	Tuesday	Wednesday	Thursday	Friday	Saturday
Lunch							
Dinner							

	Sunday	Monday	Tuesday	Wednesday	Thursday	Friday	Saturday
Dinner							

Task List

Instructions:

Task lists are a way to help you think ahead and essential when planning meals. These lists work best with just simple reminders of what needs to be completed that day. For example, on Sunday, you might cook a batch of cookies for a weekly snack, start marinating meats for 3 meals during the week and package lunches for Monday. Essentially, each day should have tasks for that given day and also tasks in preparation for future meals. Prepping for future meals is critical for successful long-term menu planning.

	Sunday	Monday	Tuesday	Wednesday	Thursday	Friday	Saturday
Tasks							

Buy Price versus Non-Sale Price

This table will take some time and energy to complete. You may need to do some research in obtaining the best "Buy Price" for your most expensive items. Use a price tracking sheet to jot down the prices of these items at different stores over time to identify the best price.

Tip: Details such as price per unit are important to consider

Instructions:

- Identify the items you spend the most money on.

- Identify the amount of each item your family uses in a year. It may be easiest to identify how much is used on a weekly basis, and multiple by 52. For example, if your household uses 2 rolls of toilet tissue in one week, you can estimate that you need 52 x 2, or 104 rolls of toilet tissue in a year.

- Find out how much each item costs when it is not on sale.

- Find out how much each item would cost at its "Buy Price" (when it is on sale and you have coupons for it if you use them).

- Calculate the total yearly cost for each item, based on its Non-Sale Price (Quantity multiplied by Non-Sale Price).

- Calculate the total yearly cost for each item, based on its Buy Price (Quantity multiplied by Buy Price).

- Calculate your total yearly savings on all items by using this equation: Non-Sale Price Per year (total) - Buy Price Per Year (total)

Item	Yearly Quantity	Non-Sale Price	Non-Sale Price Per Year (total)	Buy Price	Buy Price Per Year (total)	Non-Sale Price – Buy Price (Per Year)
Ketchup	5 bottles	$2.99	$14.95	$0.00	$0.00	$14.95
Chicken Breasts	80 pounds	$4.99	$399.20	$1.99	$159.20	$240.00
Ground Turkey	96 pounds	$4.95	$475.20	$1.99	$191.04	$284.16
Strawberries	24 pints	$3.99	$95.76	$1.50	$36.00	$59.76
Butter	10 pounds	$3.99	$39.90	$1.00	$10.00	$29.90
Toilet Tissue	6 packages	$11.99	$71.94	$5.00	$30.00	$41.94
Dishwashing Liquid	10 bottles	$1.99	$19.90	$0.00	$0.00	$19.90
Soap	50 bars	$1.25	$62.50	$0.66	$33.33	$29.17
Toothpaste	10 tubes	$3.99	$39.90	$0.00	$0.00	$39.90
Diapers	2250	$0.40	$900.00	$0.10	$225.00	$675.00
Totals			**$2,119.25**		**$684.57**	**$1,434.68**

Item	Yearly Quantity	Non-Sale Price	Non-Sale Price Per Year (total)	Buy Price	Buy Price Per Year (total)	Non-Sale Price – Buy Price (Per Year)
Totals						

Meal Price

Instructions:

Identify the main items or ingredients needed for your meal. Of course you could choose to include every single item down to the seasonings and condiments; however, I would recommend just including the main ingredients as you are learning this process. You can go back and add more details once you get the hang of it.

Fill in the amount needed for each ingredient from the recipe

Fill in the number of servings you anticipate the recipe will produce

Calculate the cost for each of the individual main ingredients.

Add up the costs for each item to identify the Total Meal Cost. Divide the Total Meal Cost by the "# of Servings" to get the cost per serving.

Use the "Category" line to fill in details such as type of cuisine or protein source. This will aid you in developing a diverse menu plan.

Example:

Meal Name: Turkey Cheese Burgers & Fries

Item	Amount	# of Servings	Cost
Ground Turkey	1.5 pounds	8	3.50
White Potatoes	2 pound	8	1.40
Hamburger Buns	8 buns	8	0.99
Cheese	8 slices	8	1.00
Total Meal Cost			**$6.89**

Total Meal Cost: $6.89

# of Servings: 8

Cost Per Serving: $0.86

Meal Name:

Category:

Item	Amount	# of Servings	Cost
Total Meal Cost			

Total Meal Cost: _____

# of Servings: _____

Cost Per Serving: _____

Made in the USA
Lexington, KY
13 January 2015